AF570753

# STEALTHY DAYS

poems by

Robert Sargent

Forest Woods Media Productions, Inc.

The Bunny and the Crocodile Press

Washington, D.C.

Copyright © 1998 Robert Sargent
All rights reserved.

International Standard Book Number: 0-938572-20-2
Library of Congress Card Number: 97-077139
First Edition published in the U.S.A.

Cover art by Mary Sargent
Painter and photographer, she lives in New York City.

Book typography by Cindy Comitz, *In Support* Graphics

Printing by George Klear, *Printing Press, Inc.*

Orders:
The Bunny and the Crocodile Press Distribution
c/o 815 - A Street, N.E., Suite #2
Washington, DC 20002

Forest Woods Media Productions Inc.
The Bunny and the Crocodile Press
Washington, D.C. 20016

For Lula, my daughter, 4, who
keeps my papers straight on the
floor where she had put them
and often, to help me, turns the
computer off without being asked.

With my greatest love.

The following poems have appeared in the following publications: "William White of Deep Creek, Virginia," *Hampden-Sydney Poetry Review*; "Lord of the Leaves," *Poet Lore*; "The Echo," "Sidney and Paul," "Nineteenth Century Photographs," and "Basie's 'How long Blues'," *Pembroke Magazine*; "July, 1931" and "Christine," *Sandhills Review*; "The Literary Pianist Speaks of his Girlfriend," *Tar River Poetry*; "The Invocation," "Reading Late On a Blowy Night" and "The Visit of the Queen," *Candelabrum*, (British); "Passing a Flowerbed," and "Finding a Poem," *Poetry East*; "Mary at the Sea of Galilee" and "Jesus and the Centurion," *Ball State University Forum*.

The following poems have been accepted by the following publications: "Botticelli's 1478 Venus" by *Candelabrum* (British); "The Pinecone" by *Hollins Critic*; "The Cold Deserted Streets of Downtown Asheville," "Mr. Geoffrey Smith...," "Fate of a Poem," and "Bix," by *Pembroke Magazine*; "A Happening at Taos" and "The Father of the Prodigal Son" by *Sulphur River Literary Review*.

# CONTENTS

## CLOSE



## NOT SO CLOSE

# CLOSE

# FINDING A POEM

*for Patrick Clary*

I am reading a poetry manuscript done by an old friend
and I come to a poem of loss, separation from a lover,
with a simple listing of things that remind him of her:
newspaper items they used to notice and comment on at breakfast,
places they went together,
the poem going through these with length of line and their number
          fittingly chosen,
the tone steady and sure,
and a fine ending trimeter, "This poem is a mistake."
I put the manuscript down, touched,
not by the sadness of the parting,
these things happen to all of us,
not feeling for him in his loneliness,
probably did him some good,
but thinking, now here is a writer, a *poet,*
and most of all here is a *poem*.

# FATE OF A POEM

I wrote a love poem once that caught my thought
when I wrote it. The poem at the time was mine.
I used it recently to conclude a reading
and touched a woman's feeling.

After the reading she came to tell me so.
Probably something in her own past was working
that fitted the poem. I liked the praise, of course,
but was feeling ironic,

my view these days: that what you see is not,
or is seldom, the full story. I finally said,
"I'll tell you a secret. Since writing that poem I've changed.
My feelings toward her, I mean.

She's not 'there' anymore." The poem had implied
she'd be there always. The woman and I agreed
about the sadness of that, but went on to talk
about poems made public, published,

as this one had been. They take on a life of their own.
I said, "The poem's not mine anymore. *You*
are now the owner." She thought about that a minute,
then said she was glad to have it.

# WILLIAM WHITE OF DEEP CREEK, VIRGINIA

My great-grantfather, mother's side, the southern.
Attended Princeton in the 1840's.
Expelled for taking a cow into his room,
"to teach the damn Yankees how to make eggnog."
Married, three children, all before the War,
which naturally he took part in, left it a colonel.
Only wounded (lucky!) in Pickett's charge.

These mythic deeds make us a little uncomfortable—
too perfect in their legendary stamp.
But something unmythical brings him a little closer:
in the 1850's he sat, one day, in the living room,
surrounded by family. The children were being quizzed
on the catechism by his wife, very religious
and half-deaf. From behind his lifted paper,
concealing his face, he gave them whispered answers.
A small gift from the past.

# THE LOGICIAN

*There are no opposites: only from those*
*of logic do we derive the concept of*
*opposites—and falsely transfer it to things.*
—Nietzsche, *The Will to Power*

Chocolate is the *opposite* of vanilla,
I felt when five, unable to analyze,
Because there were just those two at that small store,
One dark, one light, taste different.

Small with my nickel, choosing one of them,
Already ensnared with putting things in place,
Order before analysis—I didn't worry,
Licking my ice cream cone.

# LORD OF THE LEAVES

For the boy, dreaming grownupness, my how fine
the life of a forest ranger seemed, up high
in a wooden, laddered tower, lord of the leaves.
But he was never Yan of *Two Little Savages,*
an ardent nature lover, a forest haunter.
Rather he saw himself in that high tower,
small sounds of birds outside, the rustle of leaves,
surrounded by stacks of *books*, unread books,
and in that delicious and undisturbed aloneness,
reading, reading.

# ON A TRAIN

A middle aged man in a dark suit, bow tie,
is making faces across the aisle
at an infant on his mother's shoulder.
The infant giggles delightedly, gurgling.
They are enjoying themselves, each with the other.
An old lady, seeing the two, smiles in sympathy.
But the twelve year old boy, two seats back,
watching the man grimacing, blowing out his cheeks,
is disgusted at this behavior.
How *dumb* he is! he keeps thinking.
He wants to hit him, almost.

## TREES IN WINTER

A month ago, when I first came to New Hampshire,
the graveled road down which I walk to breakfast
was bounded by leafy trees,

their trunks almost invisible. Now, in the cold,
their leaves have fallen, their arching branches black
against the background sky,

distinct as individuals, each from each,
their beauty differing, aspiring or earth-seeking,
stout trunk or slender bole.

Somehow I like these more revealing views.
And suddenly I know why. I think of my father,
holding a well-loved book,

sunk in his chair, turning the pages, frowning,
comparing the photographs in his *Trees in Winter.*
His liking for the unadorned.

# THE PEDANT FROM BOSTON

*A proper Bostonian's answer to the question,*
*"Did you ever see such weather?"*

*I can say without fear of successful contradiction*
*that I never have. The weather, you know, is an*
*agglomeration of atmospheric conditions, which,*
*while it may be accompanied by physical phenomena,*
*cannot in itself be made subject to optical*
*perception.*

My father's family, being from Massachusetts,
but not from Boston, affected to despise
those Boston Brahmins, their pedantic ways,
and when my father told the weather story,
he'd assume an air pedagogical, mocking his subject,
and we were supposed to laugh at the priggish Bostonian.
But—those elegant, multisyllabic words!
Above all, their preciseness! Secretly, I admired him.

# MISS BIRDIE

Miss Birdie taught sixth. And no question about it,
she taught. A little thin wiry woman,
glaring eyes—what a change from the lax fifth!
Everyone knew that Miss Birdie was running things.
She used to sit in the back of the room,
so as to keep an eye on her fidgety charges.
When one of her pupils wouldn't speak up,
Miss Birdie would say, "Christmas is coming,"
and if anyone spoke out of turn with the wrong answer,
Miss Birdie'd glare at the culprit and say,
"Another county heard from," —pause—
and nobody elected!"
When I heard that old phrase on "Mash" recently,
I think B.J. was the one,
but only the first four words in the wrong context,
I thought of Miss Birdie, what she'd've said:
"Ignorance!"

# THE STATEMENT

I am thinking about a monosyllabic statement,
which shows a habit of mind, a point of view
that Hume and Santayana would have endorsed,
conducive to wisdom,
embodying humor and tolerance, but firmness, too,
applicable not only to deep philosophical questions
but also to many occasions arising in daily life.
I am thinking of its admirable and unadorned clarity,
and of the time when I first heard it used:
late 20's, a small Mississippi town
and a black minstrel show under a tent near Main Street,
a small jazz group to bring the people in,
the audience, black and white, sitting on divided benches,
watching the performers, men and women,
loud, humorous, argumentative,
enacting their little dramas of love and jealousy.

But now and then,
when made appropriate by some twist of plot,
a tall and black-robed man would emerge from the wings,
draw himself up, point to the struck-dumb actors
and intone the memorable statement:
"Now that may be so, but I doubt it."

## THE ECHO

As Beethoven repeats a musical phrase with a different grouping of
    instruments, giving it added significance,
and as Brubeck echoes Desmond's closing notes on the alto sax with
    the piano,
but phrasing it differently,
so Martha Ann Webb, thirteen, standing in her front yard with a
    teenage boy,
who was trying to get her to say she liked him
and pointing out they were alone, "It's just us,"
with all the resources of English to choose from,
searching for something fitting for modesty,
chose rather to whisper his closing words,
transmuting them into a touching and differing meaning,
"It's just us."

# JULY, 1931

John Boatwright, sandy-haired in overalls,
who never finished the seventh grade,
one of a group of toiling men under a blazing sun,
is digging a hole with a posthole digger, slow work,
for 25¢ an hour, ten hours a day, six days a week,
which figures out $15 a week
to bring home to his wife and children.

The college boy waterboy, lugging his bucket and dipper,
whose brother high in the company got him the job
so he'd learn what hard work is,
is trudging from workman to workman,
who're calling him over and over, "Waterboy! Waterboy!"
and slurp his water down,
"Goddamn, it's hot!"

The waterboy comes to John Boatwright,
who stops, breathing hard, and takes the dipper,
drinks deep and fills it again. He looks up and says,
"Waterboy, I went to the man for this job,
ain't nobody made me take it," grinning the while,
letting waterboy know he does what he does by choice.
And he adds, still grinning,
"It's hard but it's fair."

# THE INVOCATION

The narrow stair,
Slanted and worn, goes steeply up ten steps to this old room,
Whose bed I do not share,

On which I lie,
On a rainy day in the tenth month of a slowly ending year,
Wondering how and why

All things had led
To this small-windowed room, this bachelor's rented furnished box,
And its one single bed.

No one is here
For my support on this gray dreary drizzling day of fall,
So I must look elsewhere:

Old poets above me,
Speak to me again as you did when you brought the groaning tears:
Tell me again you love me.

## READING LATE, ON A BLOWY NIGHT

Alone, sunk in my chair, around me a hush....
then a sudden RUSH
of a cold wind! And the doorcurtain whipping, lashing,
in a furious white malevolence, bent on smashing
everything within reach! Swirling toward our vase!
I jump and jerk the curtain back in place,
slamming the door. That keeps us from that harm.
Then I go back to Dostoevsky's storm.

# CHRISTINE

Talking with Bill, he happened to notice my car,
a '71 Plymouth Duster, orange, low,
still handsome to me. I said, "That was Chris's car,
we picked it out one day—*she* picked it out.
She used a word to describe it, that, to some,
would have an opposite meaning. 'That's a *dog*!'
was what she said, admiring it." "I can hear her,"
Bill said, smiling. "And so, we naturally bought it.
You know, she had a way of getting her way
without disturbing the peace. She told me once,
her husband, her first husband, before they got married,
he was in med school in Memphis, took up with a nurse.
That disturbed Chris some. Do you know what she did?
She put on a red riding habit, got on her horse,
and rode him over to where he lived. He came out
to talk—she made the horse caper a little—prance—
had that red cap, pulled down. When she rode off
she *had* him, she told me. No more of that nurse."
"That was Chris," Bill said, chuckling. I drove off.

Other things. One day, soon after we got married,
out driving together, she hadn't yet learned D.C.,
I said, "This is Rock Creek Park." "Oh I know that,"
she said, in mock indignation. "I've been here before.
Drove all around here yesterday—by myself."
She paused for a moment, then added, "Inadvertently."

There was that time I told Roland about,
he put it in one of his poems, when she called to me
from her sick bed, to tell me something important

(she didn't have too much time), said she'd been thinking
about it for years, said "Bob, the real truth is
you never could sing worth a damn." Helpless laughter, both sides.

Had a dream last night, doubtless because of this poem,
I was telling a stranger about her, not Bill, someone else,
but anyway, in the dream, I started crying.
That woke me up. I had no tears. Pensive.
That's how I am these days, happily married,
no tears for the past, but sometimes something comes up,
like talking to Bill, and I think of the way she was.

# THE COLD DESERTED STREETS OF DOWNTOWN ASHEVILLE

Cold night of an ending year, season of Christmas,
and I left my room to walk the deserted streets
of downtown Asheville, under the yellow streetlights.
All was quiet at first and then, far off,
the sound of booming laughter, louder and louder,
as I walked on. Then rounding a corner I saw
a huge figure of Santa Claus, in a store window,
seated, red robed, laughing, his great belly
rising and falling, his right hand clapping his knee
in exuberant, feigned delight, his voice booming out
a hideous cacophony of mirth.
Up the street, down, no one was there. A block away,
a lonely car passed a corner and was gone.
And I was alone with this monster,
sending his forced and programmed laughter over
the cold and wind-swept streets. Suddenly, he froze
in mid-course, his voice ceased, his hand stopped moving,
his eyes fixed in a cataleptic glaring stare.
Then a sibilant sigh of internal mechanism,
a click, the oppressive, mirthless laughter resumed,
the belly took up its restless heaving, the hand
began rising and falling against the red garbed knee,
the red lips opened and closed in mechanical joy.
As I walked away, the loud and repetitive laughter
followed me down the deserted streets of Asheville.

## SIDNEY AND PAUL

I miss him most, Sidney, when something comes up
he would've liked, the other night for instance
when I ran into Paul, novelist now,
but once a jazz musician.

We started talking records, he mentioned Muggsy,
master of the muted trumpet, his "Sister Kate."
It turned out we'd both loved that piece for years,
one chorus especially,

the seventh and eighth bars, Brunis on the seventh,
his rich trombone straight from the Rhythm Kings,
then the whole band in *unison* on the eighth,
hitting the same notes.

We talked on.  By missing Sidney I mean
if he'd been there he would have remembered Muggsy,
would have known that unison thing, we'd all have been laughing.
Some things don't mesh in time.

# KEN

"Now you might think," Ken said, his wrinkled face,
bearded and smiling, across the restaurant table,
"those two old guys across the room, having lunch,
are talking politics since this is Washington.
Or maybe the movies or headlines, stuff like that.
You'd be wrong. Know what they're talking about?
Their *health*, that's what! How some test came out,
and what that means in terms of hospitalization.
Doctors and insurance and pills and all that shit."
I laughed, agreed. Then we resumed our talk
about doctors, insurance, pills and all that shit.

## STEALTHY DAYS

The stealthy days come on in their usual fashion,
sneaking through May, approaching the summer solstice.
By the time that comes

I will have had another late-life birthday.
Well, I say, so what! Things keep happening,
things of interest.

It was only last week I put into words my affection
for Darwin and William James—based on their openness,
their unpretentiousness.

And discoveries! My new admiration: the lovely books
designed by Leonard Baskin, now on display
at the Library of Congress.

These small epiphanies seem to me OK things.
And these stealthy days—I've never wanted to slow them,
only to fill them.

# A CERTAIN DAY

The day was sunny and fresh, we were walking together,
Bobby and I, over the Civil War battlefield,
Stones River, the Yankees call it. We call it by the town,
nearby Murfreesboro.

We traced how the battle went. "Now Rosecrans,
he'd be coming from there," Bobby said, pointing.
"Bragg would be over here, don't you think, Dad?"
As usual, I thought as he did,

agreeably together. "He had that hill to protect him,"
I added to buttress his argument. Studying the terrain,
we tried to imagine the scene, noisy with guns,
men falling in their blood.

Our talk turned to generals, which ones we most admired.
Bobby chose Thomas. "The Rock of Chickamauga," he said.
"That battle came later," I pointed out. "Yes," he said,
"but he was in there, whenever."

He continued, "Dad, do you know why I picked Thomas?
His unpretentiousness. Not the swaggering hero,
like Sheridan, say." That went way back for me,
to his grandfather's (my dad's) views

on how to behave. The remark put a crown on the day.
That he would choose that particular virtue, I mean.
This was a late March day, 1995,
about forty miles south of Nashville.

# THE RULE

There seems to be this what shall I call it rule
that people die after a while. I've seen it happen
in my own family, first my mother and father
and later my older brother. Doesn't it seem
that it might apply to me? I mean some day.
And furthermore, to strengthen that deduction,
consider that no one, born say in 1850
is alive today. *No one.* According to that
the rule is *all-inclusive.* And according to *that*
it *would* apply to me. Hard to dispute.
In spite of it being unreasonable. Might be soon.
If so, what then? I know I'll be remembered,
by those I know and love, with fondness, some.
In that sense I'll live on. The trouble is
this loathsome rule will apply to them as well.
My great-grandson will doubtless know my name
and some few facts, but his granddaughter won't.
This is a not too acceptable state of affairs.
But meanwhile, while I'm waiting, there's today,
which happens to be bright, the kind I like,
and there's a new book, also lunch with Hastings.
And that Louis Jordan CD. Mary Jane and I
will sit on the couch, listening, squeezing hands.

## 2020 AD

Lula Sargent, Chinese-American, in her twenties,
was talking to her boy friend of her childhood.
"My father, my adoptive father, I mean,
used to take me to Stanton Park, when I was two.
We lived on Capitol Hill, and it wasn't far.
No, I don't remember those trips,
I got this story from my sister Mary.
She says every day when we got to the park,
before he took me out of the stroller,
he'd sing a particular song,
'Let the Rest of the World Go By.'
First he'd sing it waltz time, you know,
one two three, one two three.
        With some one like you
        A pal so good and true.
And he'd explain it to me: 'Lula, this is waltz time.'
Then he'd shift to four beats to the measure,
and say, 'This is the beat they use in jazz.'
On this one he'd always tap his feet
And Mary says he'd be snapping his fingers on the offbeat."

"And what would you do?" her friend asked.
"Well, my dad told Mary I'd listen as if puzzled,
frowning a little,
then when he was through I'd toddle away,
as if 'Well, glad that's over!'"

# THE LEARNERS

The two of them are acting out old roles,
each playing the proper part;
old man and family infant left in his care.

He has to get the two-year-old to bed,
which entails, among his duties,
clothing her tiny body in pajamas.

She's at an early learning stage with language,
distinguishing the letters
one from another. She's only up to A.

He's at an early learning stage with infants.
Though he'd been once a father,
he'd never learned what he thought women's work.

They are sitting at the edge of a bed together. She,
naked except for diapers,
is holding a lettered picture book in her lap,

looking for A's. Those that are capitalized
she recognizes at once,
points and cries out in triumph at each discovery.

He's trying to fit her legs in the proper holes,
and then her arms, of course,
but he is a little clumsy, this old man,

and her book gets in the way, so it's not easy.
And he must tell her frequently
how smart she is to recognize those A's.

Now the pajamas are on, but must be secured
by a vertical series of snaps
up the infant's back. Oh, for a zipper! he thinks.

Each snap must be mated properly, pushed together
precisely the right way,
and the child wriggling and squirming. Hard to do!

But finally done. And next time he'd know better
how to handle the snaps.
And she'd be probably up to B's and C's.

They're smiling together, the learners. He lifts her up
and lowers her in her crib.
Good night, he says. She lies down, says good night.

## LULA AND I

You came to us, a little girl from China,
one and a half, not walking yet but about to,
didn't take long. You've been with us a year.
You're running now, and jumping and climbing, too,
but best of all, talking. Commanding, I should say.
Always, to you, the world and the people in it
are things to enjoy, including your new parents,
your new mom most of all, but Baba, too,
a name you gave to me.
                                        Your joy is contagious,
even to strangers, who sometimes stop to marvel.
When you climb in my lap to be read to, lugging a book,
I help you settle down, open the book,
start reading, you turn the pages, knowing just when to.
A congenial task!
                                When we finish, I'm usually thinking
of this my late life state, creaky, I guess,
but fortunate, too, having been given you.
Since I myself played a part in bringing you here,
I'm proud of myself. And glad.

# NOT SO CLOSE

# THE LITERATE PIANIST SPEAKS OF HIS GIRLFRIEND

She's not in the key of C, all white as snow,
like Dickens's heroines—no, she's more B-flat,
where notes of black are met with now and then,
for piquant variety, as in Thackeray's women.
And the ending of a scene with her is often
not on a tonic chord, but a major seventh,
one half-tone from peace.

## READING FINNEGANS WAKE

I don't suppose very many if any readers
read *Finnegans Wake* as I do, only a page
or two at a time, daily, with no special effort
to understand what I'm reading, skimming along,

letting the stream of words flow over me, through me,
a river of bastard language with sudden turns,
mysterious eddies, intersecting cross currents,
seemingly knowing exactly where it is going,

indifferent to what bystanders' opinions may be,
exuding a humorous charm as it rolls along.
When I close the book, I'm somehow invigorated,
like having a bracing dip in active waters.

## INNSBRUCK

I have an art card of a Durer painting
depicting the city of Innsbruck, narrow-spired buildings
surrounding a large courtyard, no people visible.
When I encounter this particular card,
I don't think of the excellence of the painting,
but rather I think that this was where Claus lived
who cast in bronze Neptune taming a seahorse.
I've heard the sculpture was thought a rarity.
And Fra Pandolf, who did a standing portrait
of the Duke's young wife, not long before she died,
may've lived here too. Both of them worked for the Duke.

# YEATS

You were master of words, how they sound, how they fit together,
and better as you got older, sure of yourself.

"The Circus Animals' Desertion," for instance. Who
could improve, or want to, its three final lines?

Or could, when describing the hour of some rough beast
for its nativity, hit on a word like "slouches"?

But such a bullshitter. All that communion with spirits,
your wife as medium. The automatic writing. Occultism.

And the book, *A Vision* you called it, aptly named.
Poopooing science. William, you should have known better.

But who can deny your talent? I'd say genius.
Auden was critical, said you were silly sometimes,

but wrote that the day of your death was a dark cold day.
Said your gift would survive it all. Your pardon, William,

I shouldn't be writing this way. But I'm irreverent,
except to my true masters, Hardy and Frost.

# READING HEIDEGGER

*Presencing, in relation to what is present,*
*is always that in accordance with which what is present*
*comes to presence.* —Heidegger, *Early Greek Writing*

I don't know what this means, the above. Then why
Do I keep on reading? Is it because it's a duty
To read an important philosopher?

Partly. But something seems more important to me
Than whatever's meant. It is Heidegger patiently trying
To recover, grasp, go back to

Ancient Greece, Aegean Miletus, pouring over
Anaximander's far-off message, weighing,
Balancing what is meant

By those few cryptic words, the surviving fragment.
I can be sympathetic to this, the effort.
But not the obfuscation.

# THE ELMS

In winter, the dark, spreading limbs of the elms,
seen against the sky,

sweep outward, upward, in graceful arcs,
as if imploring.

Led astray by romanticism, we've lost our sense
of their treeness,

their earthiness, and it's very difficult
not to see them as if

they are standing there, quietly erect, waiting
for some benediction,

with their topmost, upreaching, and delicate tracery
seemingly supplicatory.

# BOTTICELLI'S 1478 VENUS

This earlier picture has none of the charming distractions
of a fanciful Cytheran beach, or ritual actions
of lesser divinities—only the naked queen
faces us, tall and fair, outlined by that keen
and delicate Sandroan line, all gold and white
against the surrounding darkness. And on her bright
soft countenance he puts a crafty smile,
compounded of sadness and mockery, pride and guile:
sadness for pain she causes, guile concealing
her pleasure at our warm and wanton feeling,
mockery for the bigot, his poor soul,
and proud acceptance of her wicked role.

# THE PINECONE

*Now of the heaven which is above the heavens, no earthly poet has sung or ever will sing in a worthy manner.*
–Socrates, *Phaedrus*

Socrates,
please!
This evanescent ideal world of yours
whose beauty soars,
you say, so many leagues above our own,
though pleasant to meditate on, cannot be known
except in our imaginative thought,
not ours to touch and see,
no shell, no weathered rock, no arching tree,
no far-off landscape caught
between two rolling green-clad nudging peaks,
nothing that speaks
to us in its own right of simply being.

I think of Van Gough walking in a wood,
as was his wont, alone,
rough-clothed and bearded, looking, peering, seeing
things in his immediate neighborhood,
and stooping to pick up a fallen pinecone
that somehow caught his eye.
Perhaps its intricate structure? Who knows why?
He took it back to his studio, set it up
on his rough table, next to a vase and cup,
for a simple still life. Finally satisfied,
he laid out his brushes and paint, his canvas, eye'd
the objects again, and then began to paint,
swiftly, surely, apparently little restraint,

but that's a misapprehension. When he'd done,
the captured pinecone was a beauty won
from our, not your, world's stubborn entities.
This for you to think over, Socrates.

# NINETEENTH CENTURY PHOTOGRAPHS

Leaving the gallery, perhaps I should have been thinking
of all of the changes photography introduced, how
we know now the way a street looked in 1850, horse turds,
historically relevant stuff. Or perhaps
I should have been thinking about the later artistic developments,
Steichen, Evans, Christenberry, rivaling pictorial art.
Or about what it's doing to us today in movies, TV.
But instead of historical, aesthetic, sociological thoughts,
praiseworthy musings fit to impress people,
I couldn't get out of my mind the bonnetted, skirted women,
the hatted and trousered men,
how they looked at each other, sometimes at the camera,
aware of themselves as they were, just then, at the time,
and I could think only one thing, they are all dead.
All of those people are dead.

# EPITHALAMIUM

Yeats told us once, in speaking of his daughter,
And all the ways he wanted her to prosper,
Of how he hoped her bridegroom

Would bring her to a house of ceremony.
We know he favored love, but bolstered by
The magic of public rite;

Felt that, beyond their special, private feeling
Each for the other, standing before the world
Would strengthen their mutual commitment.

Margie and Mark:  surely Yeats knew well
What he was saying:  we, your family and friends,
Are glad for you and this wedding.

# A HAPPENING AT TAOS

*From a description of the hanging of several men in Taos, New Mexico, in 1847.* L. H. Garrard: *Wah-to-yah and the Taos Trail*

When the wagon was driven out from under the nameless men,
and they dropped together, jerking in the sunlight,
two of their hands touched in the aimless swinging of bodies.

And the hands of the two men gripped, held,
the slow moments passing,
until they finally loosened.

# NEW ENGLAND STATUE

The steepled skyline of New England towns,
the tended houses and the sturdy people,
suggest a strength most sobering to oppose.
I don't suppose they speak much of the War

as we still do, brought up hearing about it.
For them, the issue's settled. But here's a statue,
a Union soldier in the village square,
reminding us of what was once important.

I go up closer. "War of the Rebellion"
carved in the granite pedestal. Shows us what
New Englanders thought about it, at the time.
Also some listed names of their dead sons.

L. C. Jones was one. And Ephraim Collins.
Perhaps an Old Man Collins in this town
still speaks of his great-granddad, Ephraim,
and how he served with Grant at Petersburg.

I think of old Miss Lela and Miss Elsie,
speaking of that rascal General Sherman,
how he kept turning down their grandpa's houses.
And Mrs. Carroll's tales of the siege of Vicksburg,

how they ate dogs. The cannon Whistling Dick.
No mention of slavery, none. Instead they spoke
of "the beast of New Orleans," Ben Butler, his prostitute order.
They went to their graves that way, unreconstructed.

The voices of pride and anger are dying away.
What's left are statues like this one, cold and voiceless,
the bloodied battlegrounds, grassed over now,
and the calm historians, telling us how it was.

# THE OLD HISTORIAN

Old man at an umber table. There he sits,
Searching the evidence, as he slowly fits
Heuristic concepts to an older time,
Another country. And as poets by rhyme,
Musicians by their measures are constrained,
So all his dreamy art must be contained
By gnarly, wooden facts not trimmed or lengthened,
And by their discipline his art is strengthened.
All seems athwartways in the slanty scene
He makes for us. Familiar figures lean.
Later, we grow accustomed to his view
Of how things were, forget we thought it new.
Old crafty bearded wizard. Patient sleuth.
The erector of edifices. The inventor of truth.

# THE VISIT OF THE QUEEN

We built this fence when Her Majesty visited here,
        In Port of Spain,
So the patchwork huts would not be easily visible
To the royal eye and conscience. We don't sneer,
        In Port of Spain
At the comfort there is in avoiding a look at the miserable.

# THE ROUÉ

There was this woman I met not too long ago,
obviously looking for something, so naturally I
came on to her some—I didn't try too hard,
didn't give her the full treatment. Not too appealing.
In fact, I promptly forgot her. Then one night
I got this call, her husband was out of town,
could I come over? On this particular night,
it was after midnight. I was already in bed.
Also, tired as hell. Had already had it
once, that night, earlier. On top of that,
she lived all the way across town. Gave me a problem.
Well I figured by going I'd surely add one to the list,
an easy score—and somehow I felt I *owed* it
to men in general—not to fail them, you see?
So off I went. It was a matter of *principle*.

# A POOLSIDE LESSON

Billy Ed Baker was sitting, paunchy and fiftyish,
in a canvas poolside chair in all of his maleness,
surrounded by women and children, some swimming, some lolling
in the afternoon sun around the edge of the pool.
When Douglas, six years old, emerged from the water
dripping and panting, Billy Ed, alert to his duty,
questioned him sternly, "*Why* did you let that *girl*
beat you swimming?" Douglas, not yet fully
taught his place in our culture, conquered for him
by thousands of dads, handed down, a precious bequeathment,
was taken aback, then managed to say, with some dignity,
"I didn't *let* her—I was doing my best,"
a young man obviously needing further instruction.

## THE STARLINGS

Here is a starling hopping around in the grass,
doing a principal thing for himself, eating.
And over here is another one, hopping and eating.
Now if it occurs to one of them, maybe a male,
that the other one is—those chirps!—luckily female,
he might do another principal thing, hop and mount her,
enacting his role of fathering, furthering starlings.
Now let us think deep thoughts about these starlings.
Let us consider how very alike they seem
to us, who can hardly tell them apart, but to them—
to *them*!—how different, unique, they seem to each other.
Now let us give them the oh-so-poetic comparison:
"Oh, they are just like us! Individuals all!"
raising them, thus, from their low status to ours.
How pleasant the insight! What a compassionate view!
And what a comfortable way to think of the starlings,
of them raised up, rather than us put down.

# THE COFFEE SHOP

*The probability is practically zero that living systems,*
*which may well exist elsewhere in the cosmos, would*
*have evolved into something looking like human beings.*
—Francois Jacob, *Evolution and Tinkering,*
*Science, 10 June, 1977*

The coffee shop this morning is full of people
sitting around at the various breakfast tables,
talking together like this: "And how're your eggs?"
"Looks like a nice day, doesn't it?" Back and forth.
The elderly couple sitting across from each other
chat amiably, planning their trip. "Let's make it today
to Skyline Drive." A relaxed manner of talking.
Across the aisle, a couple, average people,
perhaps in their thirties, are speaking a different way:
she is smiling at something he said, she reaches across
the table, finds his hand, whispers an answer.
Toward the back, a waitress spits some words
angrily at the cook. Well, I'm thinking,
if not elsewhere, we are certainly here,
in all our garrulousness.

## PASSING A FLOWERBED

The proud tulip over the vulgar dandelion.
The tulip is not proud.
The dandelion is not vulgar.
They are flowers performing their roles.
No, they don't perform roles. Actors perform roles.
They are not actors, they are flowers behaving as flowers.

Again: the proud tulip over the vulgar dandelion.
The tulip isn't proud, the dandelion isn't vulgar, they are not
performing roles.
They are flowers behaving as flowers.
They are flowers in their efflorescent floralness.
Flowers.

# DEWEY

*Our sense of an essential personal flavor in each of the*
*great philosophers, typical but indescribable, is the final*
*fruit of our own accomplished philosophical education.*
—William James

From Socrates on, the philosophers want to persuade us
to think their way, their zeal barely concealed
under the careful speech, the scholarly references.
But Dewey conceals nothing. Speaking at Edinburgh,
in 1929, his Gifford Lecture,
we have only the written speech to go by, now,
and his platform appearance can't be exactly envisioned:
surely an elderly, proper man, eyeglasses,
mustache, and facing a cultured, attentive audience.
But one thing is clear, his tone:
urgent, passionate, loving, almost scolding.
Telling us to grow up.

# THE PHILOSOPHY STUDENT

She's taking philosophy now, so we inquired,
"What did you learn today?" "Today?" she said,
"Heidegger, today. You know that Van Gogh picture,
two old shoes, beat up brogans, dirty?
Well, Heidegger said they belonged to a peasant woman,
and went on and on about that. Then Meyer Schapiro,
he's a big art historian, says why does Heidegger
think they belong to a peasant? And why a woman?
In fact, Schapiro says, they belonged to Van Gogh.
Then who jumps into the fracas? Derrida does!
He says Schapiro's wrong, says how does he know
the shoes belong to Van Gogh? And why a *pair*,
they might be two *odd* shoes, just thrown together?
And why does Heidegger think they belong to peasants?
Maybe armed phantoms own them, Derrida says,
he's rolling now, that Derrida, hard to beat.
Oh, it was neat, the whole thing, those old shoes."
"So what did you learn?" we said. "Well," she answered,
"It's just like Derrida said. No truth in shoes."

# CAPITOL HILL HOUSE

Sits there in cubic solidity, three stories high,
bricked and windowed,
enduring in unpainted redness.

We can ascribe to it, if we wish,
memories of what has happened in its vicinity,
Lincoln walking by once, a stovepipe hat,
Frederick Douglass, too, dignified in black,
his home a few doors away,
Walt Whitman no stranger.

Or assume it feels pride in its location,
the Supreme Court near in a white formality,
the Capitol, too, its wide grassy lawn
laid out by Olmstead, its great trees.
Grant on his horse, indomitable.

The house, however, sits there in redness,
tends to its business:  enduring.

# WONDROUS NEWS!

Wondrous news today! We are now told,
with respect to the way our universe is expanding,
that there seems to be adequate matter, *just enough*
(molecules, atoms, quarks, stuff like that)
to slow the expansion down, gravity working.
But *not too much*—which would turn the process around,
provoke an enormous contraction, a shrinking up,
so that at some far cataclysmic time,
we would be all squunched up.
Instead, our growth will flatten, level off,
be asymtotic to zero. Things will go on.
Something to give thanks for, a happy fortuity,
the squunching danger averted,
on a wondrous day in spring.

# MR. GEOFFREY SMITH,
# BREEDER OF HORSES, SUSSEX, 1841

I had a visitor the other day,
a fine upstanding English gentleman.
Very soft-spoken. Wanted to ask me questions
about my horses. Name was Darwin. Charles,
I think he said. What he was interested in
were my breeding records, and in particular
how certain body features were preserved,
stripes on the rump, for instance, or not preserved.
Had a little notebook. Carefully wrote down
my every word. And when I said, "This one
has a peculiar hoof," he was greatly interested
and inquired about his ancestry, stallion and mare.
"What about *them*? Did they, either one, have this
peculiar hoof?" We spent an hour on that.
Just why he wanted all this, I'm not sure.
I think it concerned some theory he had.
He finally left, said if that hoof happened
again, please let him know. I said I would.
What impressed me most was not his knowledge of breeding,
though he had plenty of that, but his *civility*.
Leaving, he made me feel I'd done him some good
on whatever his project was.

# DARWIN AT WORK

If there's someone you greatly admire, long since dead,
you'd like to know how he was in his private life,
unobserved by the public,

what would he maybe be doing? Fortunately,
we do indeed have just such a glimpse of Darwin,
working, lonely and intent,

on his theory covering all biological life,
so solidly based on thousands and thousands of details.
We see him exploring a small one:

holding his finger out to a lively beetle
testing whether the greatly extended mandibles
were for ornament or pugnacity.

He can tell it better than we can:

> The male *Chiasognathus Grantii*—a splendid beetle—has enormously developed mandibles; he is bold and pugnacious; when threatened he faces round, opens his great jaws, and at the same time stridulates loudly. But the mandibles were not strong enough to pinch my finger so as to cause actual pain.
>
> *The Descent of Man*
> *Chapter X, Insects*

# BLUES FOR CHU

*Chu Berry, jazz musician, killed in an auto wreck in the 40's*

Let this be blues for Chu, something I hope he'd like:
on a hot summer night in the 30's, exact date unknown,
aboard a river boat churning the wide Mississippi, near Vicksburg,
Fate Marable's band playing
for the young white couples dancing, whirling together
(the band where Louie learned to read music),
a young white man who was listening more than dancing,
standing as close as he could in front of the band,
rapt in the music,
said to the young black tenor man, seated, front row of the band,
"Who's the best tenor, you think?"
and the tenor man looked up from his blowing,
took the reed from his mouth,
didn't say Ben Webster or Bean, as the young man expected,
instead, said, one word,
"Chu."

# BIX

A rather bumpity late 20's rhythm section,
but suddenly the cornet, very clear,
the perfectly rendered notes precise, filling the space exactly,
not Louie's soaring melodiousness and power
but a feel for each note's value, Pope not Keats,
and sometimes at the end of some lines a small up-note,
almost like catching his breath, almost his signature.

## THE SONGWRITER

*I'd rather drink muddy water, sleep in a hollow log,*
*Than to be in New York, treated like a dirty dog.*
—Blues song

Somebody wrote these words, I don't know who,
who wanted to show the urban harshness of New York.
Maybe a black blues singer, who remembers
the stories told at the family dinner table
about their great-grandfather, a fugitive slave
desperately fleeing north, hiding in swamps,
and the things he'd had to endure on his way to freedom.

## BASIE'S "HOW LONG BLUES"

That day in the late thirties, the Count took with him
only his rhythm section, that great trio,
Freddie Green, Walter Page, Jo Jones. They were all he needed
for what he wanted to do:

an extended piano solo, three minutes long,
to fit the 78 format. When he sat down
at the piano, his guys around him, he noodled the keys,
to set the tone, the rhythm,

for them to pick up on before he gave them the nod.
An eight bar blues, not twelve, each one a little different.
Single notes, mostly, in the treble, tracing the melody
backed by the left hand chords.

Simple. The rhythm behind him in soft unobtrusiveness
provided the steady unemphasized beat, always there.
No flowery runs all over the keyboard, like Tatum,
no wild excursions like Garner,

everything very much under control, restrained
by unerring aesthetic discernment—taste, it's called—
nothing excessive. The piece moved on, easily,
in all of the beauty of spareness.

Hearing this now, it's as if you are watching the sunset
and the sun had decided to show you what it could do
with no clouds around for garish ornamentation.
Leaving behind a stillness.

# JACKSONVILLE

Once you give up on immortality,
there's still a feeling you'd like to leave something behind,
a mark of your presence.

I once worked in a large southern city, not long,
in World War II. A big engineering office.
We built airfields.

Thc war over, everyone left. A few years later,
stranded between planes, I had a few hours
in this same city

and went to the building where I once worked. It now
housed a real estate agency, run by strangers.
No one to talk to.

Here was the bus stop where I used to stand waiting.
There was a girl, a co-worker, used to, too.
We liked each other

somewhat. I can't remember her name. It was southern.
And I can't remember saying good-bye when I left.
Must have, though.

I had to go back to the airport. Nothing here
for me. No mark. No trace. It was as if
I had never been there.

# BIBLICAL

# THE PROPHETS OF OLD

*He himself (man) is an artistically creating subject.*
—Nietzsche

If God is man's creation,
    As some believe him to be,
Let us not assume in our pride
    A higher degree,

But rather let us glory in our handiwork,
    Conceived by those bold
And bearded aestheticians,
    The prophets of old.

# THE AMORITE COMMANDER

*Joshua 10:12-14*

I ordered the retreat early. I had to.
Joshua was sending some of his troops to encircle us.
I remember the sun was still high, but I had hopes
that with a stout rear guard most of our force,
if they could survive till dark, could still be saved.
The Israelites doubtless were hoping
the sun wouldn't set until their bloodlust was sated.
And indeed we heard later they'd put up a prayer,
led by Joshua, to slow down the sun's setting
till their victory was complete.
                                        The slaughter, that is.
And truly it seemed, that long bloody day,
that the dark was forever in coming.

I, with a few survivors,
scrambling through underbrush, torn by thorns,
leaving our comrades dead, will always remember
the coming of blessed night.

# JERICHO'S KING, WORRYING

*Joshua 2, 6*

Bad news from across the river. The Amorite kings,
Sihon and Og, have been routed, destroyed by Joshua,
their property confiscated. What comes next?
Now, they say, he's looking toward the Jordan.
And we're just the other side. Does he eye us?

I wonder what makes the Israelites so powerful?
They have a god, Yahweh, unlike other gods,
who supports them in all they do. They even say
their leaders talk to him and receive his orders.
Imagine, talking to a god! And he might tell them,
"Jericho next!" Then, they'd have to attack us.
Yahweh brooks no rivals, no lesser gods.
He insists on standing alone. *One* god, think of it!
And that he has chosen them, the Israelites
(provided, of course, they render him suitable homage),
to be lifted above their neighbors. To be superior.
Maybe this makes them strong and formidable:
"*We* are the chosen people!" Raises morale.
Whether true or not, there's *something* on their side.

And now I've just received disturbing news,
sent me by a worthy, well-known prostitute,
Rahab her name: that she suspects two men,
recent patrons of her establishment,
to be spies of Joshua. I think we are in peril.
Maybe we'd better work to strengthen our walls.

# RAHAB

*Joshua 2, 6*

I was the madam there. When my two girls
told me about their recent customers,
I smelled a rat. I told the two young men
"I think you're Israelites, spying for Joshua.
We know he's got his eye on Jericho."
Oh, they denied it at first. But that same day
our king got word (guess how) about some spies,
and began a house-to-house search. "You'll be discovered,
I told the spies. They were frightened. Then I said,
"I could hide you, you know. What will you do for me?"
They said I would be spared and all my family,
when Joshua broke through. "Put a red cloth
on your window," they said, "to identify your house."
So I took them to my roof and hid them well,
under a pile of flax.
                                        When the search party knocked,
I told them, "The men you're searching for were here,
but left an hour ago. If you hurry, you'll catch them!"
My house sat on the wall of the city, and later,
I helped them escape, lowering them out of a window.
They got away and told Joshua how I had helped them.
He bided his time, then started that hocus-pocus,
blowing rams' horns, marching around the city.
Our people, already frightened, were now convinced
by all this noisy display, that resistance was futile.
When Joshua finally broke through, they hardly resisted,
and Joshua's men slaughtered them all—men, women and children

—except for me and my household under my roof,
with the scarlet cloth on the window.

The Israelites took us
into their camp and treated us well. Looking back,
I guess I was lucky. Smart too, you'll have to admit.
And now, I'm madam here. Business is good.
And the Israelite soldiers are generous.

# ELISHA AND THE CHILDREN

*Second Kings: 2:23-24*

Oh, the little children, Elisha!
Eaten up by bears!
Because they had mocked your baldheadedness
With taunts and dares!

Forty-two little children, Elisha!
If one or two
Had been gobbled in the she-bears' jaws,
Wouldn't that do?

# THE SON OF NUN

*Joshua 2, 6*

Hilda and I were having coffee together
in Old Town. Eight AM. Looking at poetry.
And she said, smiling, "Tell me about Joshua."
No one was near and I almost started to sing,
based on an old 78, black male quartet:

> *Joshua wa-a-a-as*
> *The son of Nun.*
> *He-e-e-*
> *neverwouldstoptilltheworkwasdone.*

But didn't—instead I told something about Joshua,
how he waged psychological war with rams' horns and marches,
something pedantic.

# SUMMIT MEETING

*Second Chronicles 9:1-12*

The Queen of Sheba came riding up to Jerusalem
to have a discussion with Solomon, subject unclear.
The official account only says, "She communed with him
all that was in her heart."

We're told that Solomon answered all of her questions,
convincing her of his wisdom, and sent her home happy,
but not before she'd praised both him and his God,
laying it on pretty thick.

The story was written up by adherents of Solomon
and shows him the great wise king, dominating a woman
of some importance, a queen, who brought rich gifts.
Good for public relations.

But some might think that what she had on her mind
was fear of the growing power of the Jewish state
if directed against her own, and how to obtain
security for her people,

and that seeing his vanity, thought that the way to proceed
was to act the weak woman, give him some personal problems
for him to be wise about, sweet talk him and thus
diminish the Jewish threat.

The standard account, of course, promoting his image
"the wisest of men," (they gave him credit for *Proverbs*),
omits her strategy. But this was no problem for her.
She could smile and go home.

# THE WRITING LESSON

*These six things doth the Lord hate; yea, seven are an*
*abomination unto Him...*
*There be three things which are too wonderful for me; yea, four*
*which I know not...*

*—Proverbs 6:16-19 and 30:18-19*

I'd like to think this true: that once, in Jerusalem,
about 300 B.C., an intense young scholar,
apprentice to an old, experienced rabbi,
was employed putting together the mass of sayings,
sententious and worldy-wise, handed down through the years,
which we know now as *Proverbs.*

He needed a brief introductory phrase for the listing:
"A proud look, a lying tongue," and so forth,
the seven "abominations." Being accustomed
to parallel phraseology: to say something once,
and then to say it again in a different way,
he thought of a way to start:

"There are seven things the Lord doth hate," was his opening,
followed by, "Yea, these things he abominates."
"Not bad," said the rabbi, "But there should be numbers in both.
Their exactness seems like truth." "I see what you mean,"
the young man said. "But I don't see exactly how.
Just to repeat seems bad."

"The secret is," said the rabbi, "go up one in number.
Then the second surpasses the first. Like this," he wrote,
"These six things doth the Lord hate—" "*Seven,*"
the young man said. "But watch," said the rabbi.
"Yea, *seven* are an abomination unto him. See?
First six, followed by seven."

The rabbi paused. "This has been done before.
How do you like it?" "I love it!" the young man said.
Now the rabbi was smiling. His teaching accepted!
And by this promising, very brilliant young man!
"Yes," he rumbled. "One of those old tricks."
The young man was thinking hard.

"This can be useful," he said, "For *any* list.
Start with one less than the number. I'm thinking about
those things most wonderful Agur talks about:
an eagle, a serpent, the way of a man with a maid.
There's another, four in all. Use three, then four!"
"You've got it," the rabbi said.

# JESUS AS A PERFECT TRIANGLE

*Matthew 22:15-22*

The YMCA secretary moved closer.
I was 12. We were in his room, alone.
"Jesus was not," he was teaching me, "only spiritual.
Oh, he had mental power beyond belief.
You take that time when his great enemies,
the Pharisees, were trying to trick him, ruin him.
They egged him on, trying to get him to say
his followers shouldn't pay taxes. Then, of course,
they could have him arrested." He was squeezing my shoulder.
"But Jesus said, 'Bring me a penny.' They brought him one.
'Whose picture's on this penny?' he said to them.
'Caesar's' they said. Now—Robert, get this—"
his face was close to mine. "He said to them,
'Render unto Caesar the things that are Caesar's,
and to God the things that are God's.' He had them there!
All they could do was marvel, leave him alone!
A giant in mental power. And one more thing.
He didn't scorn the *body*. Remember that.
Spiritually, mentally, physically, he was supreme.
Three sides to him. A perfect triangle."
He leaned over to kiss me, open-mouthed,
a habit with boys he got fired for, later.

# MARY AT THE SEA OF GALILEE

*Matthew 12:46-50; Luke 2:41-52*

I think they may have to do this, sons who break away from
their parents to become themselves,
this one I worry about, he's so extreme in his views, in his
preaching I fear for him,
he offends so many, the established leaders, they try to turn
the Romans against him, he may come to harm.
Our friends fear for him, some say he has lost his mind,
last week they tried to reach him, reason with him, he didn't
listen.
And now today, in this large crowd of his listeners, he
rejected his family, rejected me,
he was told his mother was here, and his brethren,
and all he would say was, waving toward his disciples,
*here* are my mother and brethren.
I must be patient, he was always a son with a mind of his
own.
I remember that time we took him, aged 12, to Jerusalem,
and found him later disputing with doctors in the temple,
acting as if he knew all about those subjects, oh! asking and
answering questions as if he belonged there!—
what a son! Some day he may need me. I will be there.

# JESUS AND THE CENTURION

*Matthew 8:5-13*

When these two met, they must have judged each other
correctly enough, though reared in different ways.
The centurion had a servant,

Sick, needed help. From what he'd heard, he thought
Jesus could cure him, and didn't hesitate
to ask him if he would.

Jesus said yes, that he would come and heal him.
The centurion thought that this was unnecessary.
He could judge power in others.

"Like you, I'm a man of authority," he told Jesus.
When I say 'Go' to one of my soldiers, he goes.
When I say 'Come', he comes.

If you tell me my servant is cured, I believe it.
And you don't have to visit me to cure him."
Jesus was pleased at this,

and when the other got home, the servant was cured.
What comes through is the mutual respect, two men
who understood each other.

# THE FATHER OF THE PRODIGAL SON

*Luke 15*

I am an old man now and looking back
they're some things I'd do different— I don't think
I'd kill the fatted calf for my son Jude,
that time when he came home from a wastrel life,
his inheritance frittered away. His brother Ike
complained, at the time—no fatted calf for him,
who'd stayed at home and worked for my support.
And I don't blame him for that, nor didn't then.
The younger was my favorite, I admit.
I had a blind eye for his derelictions,
which didn't stop on his return. Truth is,
he wasn't worth a damn, then or ever—
lazy, shiftless, conning on his brother.
Died in jail, put there for robbing a neighbor.
Instead of falling on his neck, back then,
I'd greet him kindly stern, put him to work,
hope for the best, though that was always dubious.
And give more recognition to his brother,
who's now my main delight in my old age.
I think I'm lucky to have one good son.

## NOTES

"Lord of the Leaves": Yan is the young boy protagonist of that wonderful book for young nature lovers, *Two Little Savages*, by Ernest Thompson Seton, published 1911.

"The Philosophy Student": the criticisms of Heidegger by both Schapiro and Derrida concerning Van Gogh's painting is set forth in Allan Megill's *Prophets of Extremity,* pp 174-5.

"Mr. Geoffrey Smith, Breeder of Horses...": the encounter described in the poem is fictional but we know Darwin frequently consulted English breeders of domestic animals while working on his theory.

This is Robert Sargent's sixth book of poems. His previous books are *Now Is Always the Miraculous Time, A Woman from Memphis, Aspects of a Southern Story, Fish Galore,* and *The Cartographer.* He is a longtime member of the Washington, DC, poetry community, and was awarded the 1996 Columbia Merit Award by the Poetry Committee of the Greater Washington, DC, Area for outstanding leadership in community poetry affairs. His other interests include art and jazz.